Drawn
By The
Father

Great Christian Books
Lindenhurst, New York

Drawn
By The
Father

JAMES WHITE

A GREAT CHRISTIAN BOOKS publication
Great Christian Books is an imprint of Rotolo Media
160 37th Street Lindenhurst, New York 11757
www.GreatChristianBooks.com   (631) 956-0998
email: mail@greatchristianbooks.com
Drawn By The Father
ISBN 0-9670840-0-8

White, James, 1963-
Drawn By The Father / by James White
p. cm.
A "A Great Christian Book" book
GREAT CHRISTIAN BOOKS an imprint of Rotolo Media
ISBN 0-9670840-0-8 (pbk.)
Dewey Decimal Classifications: 200, 230
Suggested Subject Headings:
1. Religion—Christian literature—Christianity &
Christian theology
2. Christianity—The Bible—Soteriology
I. Title

Book and cover design for this title are by Michael Rotolo.
Body text is typeset in the Minion typeface by Adobe Inc. and
is quality manufactured in the United States on acid-free paper.
To discuss the publication of your Christian manuscript or out-
of-print book, please contact Great Christian Books.

**MANUFACTURED IN
THE UNITED STATES OF AMERICA**

Contents

Introduction   **9**

1 **The Bread From Heaven**   **13**

2 **Given by the Father to the Son**   **29**

3 **Christ and the Christian**   **43**

4 **The Son Doing the Will of the Father** **53**

5 **Human Inability**   **65**

6 **Conclusion**   **79**

  Endnotes   **87**

All that the Father gives Me will come to Me, and the one coming to Me I will never cast out....No man is able to come to Me, unless the Father, who sent Me, draws him, and I will raise him up at the last day."

Introduction

Before We Listen to the Words of Christ...

This is a book primarily for Christians who truly feel that the Bible is the Word of God, that it has supreme authority in the life of the believer, and that there is no higher priority in one's life than to glorify God by being obedient to what He has revealed in Scripture. Those who do not bow to the authority of the Word, or feel it to be simply a moral guide, will derive little more than a glimpse into a world unknown and unknowable until that rebellion of the heart that causes one to sit in judgment upon the written Word of God is removed. But for the believer who truly wishes to be pleasing to God by knowing God's Word and believing *all* that is revealed therein, this is an invitation to set aside the cares and distractions of the world and to sit for a blessed time at the feet of the Master by listening closely and intently to what He says about salvation— the Father's will, the Son's own promises to His people, and man's role in God's eternal plan. The words of Jesus are clear and plain; His teaching is straightforward and easily understood. It is the Christian's great pleasure to be blessed with this revelation from on high, this glimpse into the working of the Father, the Son, and the Spirit as the one triune God brings about His eternal counsel and will.

The sixth chapter of the Gospel of John, like the eighth, tenth, fourteenth, and seventeenth chapters, gives us a brief, and glorious look into the relationship of the Father and the Son. But in this, the longest chapter in the Gospel of John, the Person of Jesus Christ is the central focus. In the reflection of His majestic person, the Lord Jesus speaks of the inability of the unbeliever to understand His Person, His mission. In so doing He provides to us some of the plainest, clearest teaching on the foundational issues of the Gospel of peace. He speaks of the Father's giving of men unto the Son; and the Son's obedience to the Father in bringing *all* that have been given to Him to eternal salvation. In response to the crowd's disbelief, Jesus also gives forth a clear explanation of their inability to understand, and their inability to come to Him as the one and only source of spiritual life.

These words of Christ have always been the possession of Christ's Church. Sadly, however, there have often been *long* periods of time during which the truths that are here so clearly presented have been ignored. And no wonder! The words of the Lord Jesus are *highly offensive* to those who refuse to cling *only* to Christ— those who willfully attempt to gain God's favor by their works, their own supposed righteousness and ability. But in God's time He sends His grace to soften the hearts of man, and in so doing, the wonderful truths of this passage of Scripture are again understood, accepted and loved.

You are invited to stop and ponder for a while the great work of the Father and the Son in the salvation of God's people. Take your Bible, shut out the clamor of the world, and seek the truth of God with us. It is a great privilege to be able to listen again to the words of Jesus our Lord. Let us thank Him for His grace.

Our Loving Lord—

We thank you for creating us and giving us life. We acknowledge you to be our Creator, our Maker. You hold all things in the palm of Your hand, And we are but dust in comparison with You. But You have loved us, and provided salvation for us. We know that apart from You we can do nothing. We need Your Spirit, we need Your guidance, We must be enlightened, for our minds are so dark without You. We desire to understand the life-giving words of Christ That were recorded by the Apostle John so long ago. Bless us with your Holy Spirit, and help us to remove from our thinking all that is displeasing in Your sight. Teach us with the living words of Christ, Oh God. We thank You and praise You in Christ's name.

Amen.

1

The Bread From Heaven

Wherefore, the Lord, about to give the Holy Spirit, said that Himself was the bread that came down from heaven, exhorting us to believe on Him. For to believe on Him is to eat the living bread. He that believes eats; he is sated invisibly, because invisibly is he born again.
—Augustine

The Apostle John was a tremendously gifted writer and communicator. Those who have spent any time dealing with his masterful Gospel are constantly amazed at the depth and richness of his writing. Grammatically, he is basic and simple; yet, in his simplicity, he crafts detailed pictures of the Lord Jesus,— beautiful, flowing, dramatic. He delights in using basic, everyday words in two different ways. He plays terms off of one another, and by so doing passes on to his reader tremendous spiritual truths. In his Gospel men hear, but don't hear; they see, but they don't see; they believe, but they don't believe. Each passage must be taken on its own, yet each must be seen in the light of others. For most of us, his work is an amazing tapestry of words that is ever new. We are drawn back again and again, always delighted to find a new truth, a new aspect to the teachings of the Lord Jesus Christ.

The sixth chapter of this Gospel, the longest in the book, forms one great story, one great truth. Yet John communicates this truth to us through two stories, and then a narrative of Jesus' teaching in the synagogue at Capernaum. First comes the miraculous feeding of the five thousand, and then the storm at sea with the coming of the Lord, walking upon the water. Both stories provide the background for the teaching of Christ found in verses 26 through 65. The provision of bread in the desert in the feeding of the five thousand leads Jesus to speak of Himself as the bread of life. The crowd's seeking after signs, miracles, food and political power forms the backdrop of one of the greatest expositions of the Person and work of Jesus Christ,— and that from His own lips!

We must seriously consider these background issues so we do not "come in on the middle of the conversation" so to speak when we focus our attention on verses 35 through 45.

Often John gives little statements about the timing of certain events that we can often easily miss without proper notice. He will narrate events, and then, almost as an afterthought, mention something that is quite important about *exactly when* something happened. For example, in John 5, Jesus heals the paralytic by the pool of Bethesda. Then John gives us the important information that this took place on the Sabbath day (John 5:9). The rest of the chapter tells us the story of the conflict between Christ and the Jews due to His performing this act of mercy on the Sabbath.

In John Chapter 6, an important piece of information is given to us when John writes, "Now the Passover was near— the feast of the Jews" (John 6:4). Is this just a bit of colorful information, or is it important? Given all the symbolism that the Lord is going to utilize in the rest of the chapter, both in His actions and in His words, it seems to be an important fact. Here, at the Passover time, Jesus speaks of the true Passover lamb— Himself— and the true path to life, that of faith in Him. Rather than feasting in Jerusalem, Jesus invites people to a feast upon Himself, the bread of heaven. Furthermore, why are these people not going up to Jerusalem for the feast? These people, who start out so militant in their desire to follow Christ end up abandoning Him in light of the strong statements he makes about Himself that they later hear. Could it be that John is showing us that these people are simply superficial followers rather than true disciples, for they do not even maintain loyalty to the Passover feast itself, but instead seek after what is flashy and exciting?

Of course, John could simply be remembering the specific time-frame in which this took place. Given that the next chapter begins with the Feast of Tabernacles though, (which took place nearly six months *later*), it seems safe to assume that John wishes us to keep the Passover season in mind in listening to the words of Jesus.

Miracles with a Message

Two miracles are recorded for us in the first twentyfive verses. First, Jesus, seeing the great crowd that is coming toward Him, asks His disciples a question. "Where will we buy bread in order that these may eat?" He asks

(John 6:5). But John, in hindsight, adds that Jesus had a purpose in His question, for He Himself knew what He was about to do. None of the disciples think of the sufficiency of Christ to meet their need; their minds turn instead to worldly methods of finding sufficient food for the crowd. Andrew knows of a boy with five barley loaves and two fishes, but his speech betrays that he is desperate at this point and doesn't really think that Christ can do anything with such a small amount of provision.

What happens is known to almost everyone who has attended Sunday School or read more than a few pages of the Bible. Jesus gives thanks to the Father for the food, breaks the bread, and distributes it to all who are there— 5,000 men, and all their women and children. Jesus distributes bread to all who come to Him. He meets their need by His own sufficiency. This was not just some flashy show on Christ's part, it was the object lesson that will be explained the next day in Capernaum. Christ knows the future, and is working the will of His Father with perfect precision. When the men see this sign from Christ, they have a surface faith, and exclaim, "This is truly the Prophet, the one coming into the world" (John 6:14). But they are looking only at how they themselves can be benefited, for Christ knows that they are planning to come and to make Him king by force. To quell this popular movement, He retires into the mountain by Himself.

We can almost see the bewildered disciples as they watch Jesus walking away, climbing higher into the mountain. They surely knew the feelings of the crowd. Isn't this the perfect time for Jesus to make His identity as Messiah public, and use this large force to liberate Israel? They must have been disappointed to see their Master turning His back upon such popular sentiment and on such great acclaim. How would they explain this to those who were asking?

It seems that the crowd settles in for the night in that place, for we shall see later that they will find boats and follow Jesus across the sea the next day. The disciples go down to the sea and decide to cross over to Capernaum. Perhaps they are confused, not understanding what Christ has done, or where He has gone. Had Jesus left instructions for them to go to Capernaum? Had He mentioned going there earlier, before the miraculous feeding, and now they were heading in that direction, hoping to find Him there?

Had they waited as long as they could before beginning the dangerous journey in the dark, expecting Him to come down from the mountain and join them? We cannot tell for sure. Certainly their minds were greatly tossed about, just as the coming storm would soon toss their bodies! It had been a long, exhausting day, filled with emotional ups and downs. Still, late that night, with an evidently contrary wind, they set out in a small boat venturing toward the opposite shore of the Sea of Galilee.

As is common in desert climates, a "great wind" came up suddenly. These strong fishermen had hardly advanced halfway across the lake by the fourth watch (Mark 6:48), so they were obviously struggling hard! Physically tired and emotionally drained from the miraculous events and, to their minds, strange actions of their Lord, they toiled at the oars. Then, in the midst of the raging sea, they are shocked at the sight of a man walking upon the water. It is Christ! This event so impressed all the disciples that it is recorded in three of the four Gospels.[1]

The Lord speaks to His frightened disciples, saying, "I am— be not afraid." The English translation hides from us a significant aspect of the Lord's words. Throughout the Gospel of John the same Greek phrase[2] translated "I am" is found in very important contexts. Jesus is the "I am" before Abraham comes into existence

(8:58); He is the "I am" who knows the future (13:19, compare Isaiah 43:10); when He speaks these words their power topples those who have come to arrest Him (18:5-6); and to reject that He is the "I am" results in dying in sin (8:24). The phrase was used in the Greek translation of the Old Testament as another name for Yahweh, the God of Israel[3]. So here the Lord of creation walks upon the sea, and comforts His disciples with His reassuring words.

Christ's walking upon the water, and then His self-identification as deity, point to Himself as the Master of Creation itself. Both miracles show the deity of Christ; both miracles show the control of creation by the Lord; both point to Christ, one as the all-sufficient provider, the other as the merciful rescuer of His people; the one who finds no barrier capable of keeping Him from accomplishing His purpose in saving those who are His. We shall see these themes again in the discourse in Capernaum.

Directing the Discourse

The miracle-seeking multitude finds transportation across the sea, and quickly finds the Lord at Capernaum. John does not tell us that the ensuing dialogue takes place in the synagogue until the main section of the discourse is complete (6:59). Jesus goes to the place of worship in the morning, and it is there that He encounters these would-be followers with His own teaching concerning Himself. It is always in the context of worship that God's truth is most clearly seen.[4]

The crowd is interested in small things — like the mode of transportation Jesus used to get to Capernaum. Christ does not satisfy their thirst for trivial information, but goes immediately to the heart of the matter. "You seek Me not because you saw the signs, but because you ate of the bread and were filled" (John 6:26). We can best understand the reference to "seeing" the signs in the typical way John uses such terms as seeing and hearing— in the sense of "understanding." They were not seeking Christ because they had understood the miracle (sign) of the bread, but because they were seeking sustenance, food, free bread. They were seeking the benefits of Christ without seeking Christ Himself. Christ warns them against the foolishness of this kind of life. "Work not for the bread which perishes but for the bread which abides unto eternal life, which the Son of Man will give to you; for this one the Father, even God, has sealed" (6:27). Christ seeks to correct their errant desires; they are looking only at the physical, not at their greatest need, which is spiritual. He contrasts the temporary satisfaction which comes from the bread"that perishes" with the eternal life provided by the bread which He gives to men. God Himself, the Father, has set His seal upon the Son of Man, manifestly guaranteeing the truthfulness of His words and His promise.

The Lord's use of the term "work" in verse 27 prompts a question of the people. "What must we do in order that we might work the works of God?" They do not seem to follow what Jesus has just said, and instead seem to be asking how they also might "work the works of God," miraculous works that clearly the Lord Jesus ably performed. They continue to look past Him to other issues— but the Lord will not allow this to continue. He stops them dead in their tracks.

"This is the work of God: that you believe in the one whom He sent" (6:29). The Lord continues to point back to Himself. Does one wish to do what is pleasing to God? Does one wish to work the works of God? Then one must believe in Christ, for this is the first and foremost action that must be taken by the one who seeks to do God's will. We must often be reminded of how *radical* were these words! We often become rather accustomed to hearing this kind of talk from Christ, but can we imagine the impact upon those who first heard these words? No prophet in Israel had ever dared utter such language! None had ever pointed to himself the way the Lord Jesus points to Himself! This is no mere prophet or teacher who is speaking!

The people catch onto Christ's meaning quickly, for their next words are a challenge to Him. "What sign do you do, in order that we may see and believe you? What do you work? Our fathers ate manna in the wilderness, just as it has been written, *He gave them bread from heaven to eat*" (6:30-31). The Jews seek signs, as Paul said (1 Corinthians 1:22), and they do so here as well. Though they had seen the miracle the day before, this is not enough. Their fathers had received manna for many years. Jesus will have to do more than a one-time evening meal to compare to the miracle of the manna in the wilderness. They are again, clearly, missing the majesty of the Person to whom they are speaking, as well as the significance of the bread that Jesus is speaking about. They are stuck on physical things, while Christ is speaking of *spiritual* things. They desire to compare Christ to Moses; the Lord wants to show them something greater. "Moses did not give you the bread from heaven, but My Father is giving you the true bread from heaven, for the bread of God is the one coming down from heaven and giving life to the world" (6:32-33). No comparison between the Son and Moses is possible, for not only was it not Moses who gave the bread in the first place (it was the Father), but the bread that the Father is now giving is not simply a mysterious substance that falls from heaven, but is an actual person, a divine person, one who comes down out of heaven and who gives life to the world.

The Bread of Life: John 6:35

Life for the world? That sounds wonderful! "Always give us this bread!" they cry. But they are not prepared (though they certainly had fair warning) for Jesus' reply— "*I am the bread of life. The one coming to Me will not hunger, and the one believing in Me will never thirst.*" Jesus makes the direct connection— the bread from heaven is Jesus Christ Himself; it is not a physical food, but a life-giving person.

That Christ has from the beginning been intending to point His hearers to Himself as the source of all spiritual life is plain from the language He uses. The hunger and thirst that He satisfies is not a physical hunger or a physical thirst. Instead, the one who "hungers after righteousness" is the one who finds satisfaction in Christ Jesus. There is no limit to the supply of spiritual food that can be provided by Christ the Lord. His is a never-ending store of satisfaction for all who hunger and thirst for truth and righteousness. Coming to the Son, believing in the Son— both are referring to the same thing. These are not physical actions. When Christ speaks later about eating His flesh and drinking His blood, He clearly is not talking about actually eating flesh or drinking blood[5] but is referring back to the symbols of food and drink that are presented here. Eating and drinking is the same as coming and believing. When we eat and drink, we are changed by what we eat and drink. We derive sustenance from those things. There is an intimate relationship between the one who eats and that which is eaten! So it is with Christ. When we come to Him, when we believe on Him, He becomes the source of our spiritual life. Christ is all for the Christian, who will never seek to "snack" at the table of another when he is fully satisfied with Jesus!

Throughout this passage an important truth is presented that again might be missed in many English translations. When Jesus describes the one who comes to Him and who believes in

Him,[6] He uses the present tense to describe this coming, believing, or, in other passages, hearing or seeing.[7] The present tense refers to a *continuous, ongoing action*. The Greek contrasts this kind of action against the aorist tense, which is *a point action*, a single action in time that is not ongoing. Many "believe" in Christ in this way in John's Gospel, but they do not *really believe* because their faith is not ongoing, it is not alive. The wonderful promises that are provided by Christ are not for those who do not truly and *continually* believe. The faith that saves is a living faith, a faith that always looks to Christ as Lord and Savior. Only God can give this kind of faith to a person. It is a work of Christ in the heart.

Many in our world today want us to believe that we can accept Christ simply as a Savior from sin, but not as Lord of our lives. They teach essentially that a person can perform an act of believing on Christ *once*, and after this, they can fall away even into total unbelief and yet still supposedly be "saved." Christ does not call men in this way. Christ does not save men in this way. The true Christian is the one *continually* coming, *always* believing in Christ. Real Christian faith is an ongoing faith, not a one-time act. If one wishes to be eternally satiated, one meal is not enough. If we wish to feast on the bread of heaven, we must do so all our lives. We will never hunger or thirst if we are *always coming* and *always believing* in Christ. He is our sufficiency. Christ is the bread from heaven. We must feed on *all* of Christ, not just the parts that we happen to like. Christ is not the Savior of anyone unless He is their Lord as well. The *Lordship of Christ* will be seen over and over again in the following verses.

Seen, But Not Believed: John 6:36

Christ has proclaimed Himself the bread of life. His actions in feeding the five thousand the prior day should have communicated this to any who were spiritually sensitive, spiritually alert. But the sign did not bring faith. Jesus openly proclaims the truth about His Person but then goes on to say, "But I spoke to you because you have seen Me and yet have not believed." Christ speaks plainly and openly to the people, for it is obvious that the sign alone did not communicate truth to the people. They have not believed on Christ even though they have seen His power. He provided to them bread in a miraculous fashion, yet He rejected their political, earthly aspirations. But they did not come to true faith in Him on the basis of having seen His miraculous events. It is interesting to note that in verse 40, after the roles of the Father and the Son in the Gospel have been clearly presented, Christ will speak of the one who "looks upon" the Son as the one who has eternal life.[8] Here the people have *seen* Christ, but have not really *looked* on Christ. In both places, the operative factor is *faith*. Here, those who are not the Son's do not believe, though they have seen. Their sight is not joined to real, living faith. But those who are given to the Son by the Father (6:37) look on Christ— not simply as a miracle worker or great teacher, but as the source of spiritual life, the Son of God Himself. *They* are the ones who have eternal life.

Why do some see and yet not believe? Why do others see and believe? Are those who believe "better" than those who do not? What makes the difference? The Lord Jesus will answer that question in verse 37.

2

Given by the Father to the Son

I ask in their behalf; I do not ask in behalf of the world, but in behalf of those whom You have given Me, for they are Yours. —*John 17:9*

Unbelief

The Christian heart hates the world and what it represents. We desire to believe. We desire to trust. But many— indeed, most— of our fellow men in this world live in unbelief. Their entire view of the world is based upon a rejection of the claims of Jesus Christ, and disbelief in His Person and His work. Why? Why does the Christian heart long for Christ while others hate Him and use His name as a curse? Why does the believer hate sin while others revel in it? Why do we long for God's grace while others do not even have a sense of their desperate need?

God

God's choice, God's will, God's sovereign purpose. It is solely God's grace that makes any man to differ from another man. The best Christian is what he is solely because God has willed to gift him with goodness. The most moral, kind, gentle unbeliever is moral, kind and gentle solely because God, in His common grace to all men, has seen fit to make them that way. The Father is working out His plan in this world.

"All that the Father gives Me will come to Me." So Jesus taught the people in the synagogue in Capernaum. The Lord was pointing to Himself as the sole source of true spiritual sustenance and life. He demonstrated this in the miraculous feeding of the five thousand. Yet, these people had seen but they did not believe. Why? In verse 36 Jesus begins to explain the terrible condition of unbelief. We shall examine His words very closely, for upon the completion of this section of His discourse (6:35-40) the Jews would grumble at the claims of Christ.

Why did they grumble? What caused them offense? Let us look to the words of Christ to understand.

Initial Exegesis

"All that the Father gives Me will come to Me." We will look at each term in this first clause of verse 37 very closely.[9] But we must first provide a framework of understanding so that we can see how these words relate to one another. We shall present an interpretation, and then demonstrate through an examination of the text how this interpretation is derived. We feel that the suggested interpretation is *forced* upon us by the plain meaning of the text.

Christ is not speaking of theories here. He asserts plainly, without equivocation, that all that are given to Him by the Father will come to Him. Clearly we see here the complete sovereignty of God as the owner (since He is the Creator) of all men. He is free to give men to the Son as their Lord and Savior. What is also clearly presented is the simple fact that if God the Father gives a man to the Son, that man *will come to Christ in faith*. There is no contingency here, no possibility of this not coming to pass. The Father gives men to the Son for the express purpose of their salvation, and, because they are so given by the Father, they *will* be saved.

The inarguable truth of Christ's words is that men who are the object of God's grace in being given by the Father to the Son will come to Christ as Lord. They will do this without fail. No man who is so given will seek his salvation or his sufficiency anywhere but in Christ.

In all of this the complete rulership of God is manifest. The Father is the one who gives. His action is the primary cause, His action must be first. Nothing is said in Scripture about the Father's giving of people as being based upon anything in or of those people themselves. In fact, such an idea would be exactly opposite of what the Lord is saying. Christ is explaining the unbelief of the men who are standing before Him. Why do they disbelieve? Because they are not of those who have been given to Him by the Father.[10] The Father's choice results in man's acceptance of Christ's claims, or otherwise, by default, man sinfully rejects Him.[11] Man's actions will never determine God's decisions; God's decrees rule over the decisions of the creature, mankind.

"All"

All that the Father gives to the Son will come to the Son. All. Every one.[12] There is no doubt, no hesitation in the Lord's words. All that the Father gives Him will come to Him. There will be no stragglers, none who are called will fail to come to Christ. All. Complete unity. Every single one of those who are given to the Son by the Father will come to believe and follow Jesus Christ as Lord.

Do we accept Jesus' words? The crowd who listened, by and large, did not. But do we? Do we understand all that underlies the Lord's words? By examining the rest of this short, nine-word phrase,[13] we will be forced to consider how willing we are to believe His teaching.

"The Father Gives"

The Father is Lord of all, Creator of heaven and earth, the eternal Sovereign, the only true God. As Creator, He is the owner of all that exists. It is His right to do with His creation as He sees fit. As owner of all things, including all men, He gives men unto the Son. This is a gift of pure love for the Son, and love for those who are so given.

The concept of God as Sovereign meets universal resistance from men. Why? Because it is the one, basic fact of our existence (God is God, we are not) that we *must* reject if we are to maintain our sinful rebellion against God.

Any man who sins against God must, in so doing, deny that God is his Creator, his Master. If we all *truly* believed that God made us, that every breath we take comes from His hand, we certainly would not impudently disregard His laws and blaspheme His name by our words and our actions! Since, however, we in fact do just that, we show that we are setting ourselves up as "gods," pushing the Creator off His throne (we think) and rejecting His will for our lives. Paul describes this basic aspect of man's rebellion in Romans 1:21-25, and points out that man, in his foolish sinfulness, worships and serves the creation rather than the Creator!

Because this is part of our sin, we find those passages in Scripture that clearly portray God's absolute ownership of all of creation— including mankind— particularly disturbing to us. For example, the illustration of the potter and the clay is quite offensive to any man whose heart has not been subdued by the Spirit of God.[14] Israel is described as a lump of clay in the hands of God in Jeremiah 18:6, and the same illustration is used by the Apostle Paul in Romans 9, where he answers the charges of men against the righteousness of God in choosing some for salvation, and bypassing others, leaving them in their sinful condition (Romans 9:19-24).

But these passages exist, and if we truly desire to follow Christ, we must be obedient to His Word— *all* of His Word.

The Father gives men to the Son. This is not the only place where this truth is proclaimed. In Christ's "High Priestly Prayer" of John 17, the fact that the disciples were disciples because the Father had given them to the Son is seen more than once.

> "Father, the hour has come. Glorify Your Son, in order that the Son may glorify You. Just as You gave Him authority over all flesh, in order that He might give eternal life *to all that You have given to Him* (John 17:1-2). (emphasis added)

To whom does Jesus give eternal life? We know that all who believe in Jesus Christ receive eternal life. But prior to man's action of believing comes the Father's action of giving those men who *will* believe to the Son. Christ's authority extends over *all flesh*, but the gift of eternal life is given only to those who the Father *has given* to the Son.

> "I manifested Your name *to the men whom You gave Me* out of the world. They were Yours, and *You gave them to Me*, and they have kept your word (John 17:6). (emphasis added)

Jesus made the Father's character and purposes[15] known to His people. These men were given to the Son "out of the world." Clearly then, this is a distinct group of men *separate from the entire mass of humanity.* God the Father owns all men, the entirety of humanity, and yet *out of* the whole world He gives those individuals whom He calls *the elect*[16] to the Son. The *only* thing that separates a disciple of Christ from "the world" is the sovereign choice of the Father. But note as well the result of this decision by the Father— *they keep the words of Christ.* This is the thought that is found in the passage we are examining in John 6. Those who are given by the Father come to the Son in John 6:37; those who are given by the Father to the Son keep the Father's words in John 17:6.

In John 17:9-10 the same thought is presented:

> "I ask on their behalf; I do not ask on behalf of the world, *but of those whom You have given Me, for they are Yours*, and all things that are Mine are Yours, and all things that are Yours are Mine, and I have been glorified in them. (emphasis added)

The Lord explicitly limits the scope of His intercession as High Priest in this glorious prayer *to the elect* in clear distinction from *the world.* The prayer He offers here He offers for those that the Father has given to Him *and for them alone.*

Finally, we are almost overwhelmed by the Lord's statement in the 24th verse of John 17, when He prays—

"Father, I desire that they also, the ones you have given to Me, might be with Me where I am, so that they may look upon My glory.

The Son's loving desire for His people, those that the Father has given Him, is that they might be with Him where He is. And what is the privilege of these people? They are allowed to behold, to look upon, the glory of the Son! Surely the lost cannot possibly understand what this means to the heart of the Christian! What could be so wonderful about looking upon the glory of Christ? The believer knows, for Christ is his all. Which brings us back to John 6:37...

"To Me"

We have already emphasized that the giving of the elect by the Father is an action undertaken in love— love for the Son by the Father, love for the elect by the Father. But realize the tremendous truth that is here proclaimed. We have been given unto the Son. We have been committed into His care! The great Second Person of the Trinity has received us from the hand of the Father! The Father loves us with an everlasting love, and certainly one who loves another will not trust just anyone to care for the object of his love! But the Father knows the Son, and knows the Son's perfect and powerful ability to care for the elect.

"Shall Come"

What is the result of the divine transaction? What does the Father's sovereign choice mean in the lives of men? The answer is clear: those who are given by the Father to the Son *shall come* to the Son. It is not said that they *might* come, or that they have a higher probability than others to come, but that *they shall come*. They will come to Christ, they will believe in Christ, they will trust Christ.

Coming to Christ involves faith.[17] Obviously, then, Jesus is teaching that human faith follows after the decree of the Father; that is, those who are the Son's *will*, without fail, believe, and believe truly, in the Son. They will come to Him as the spring of eternal life, and will always seek from Him the water of eternal life.[18]

The ramifications of the Lord's words are far-reaching indeed! It is often the case today that the Gospel is presented as little more than a "plan" for your life that God has set in place whereby man, by the act of his own will, makes the right "decision[19]" ,"does" the proper things, undergoes the appropriate rituals, and by doing so, makes the plan "work." Without the individual's cooperative actions, the plan is, in reality, useless, and then when we also consider the idea that the plan is supposedly for every single human being (as contrasted with the distinction between the "world" and the "elect"), then it must be concluded that the entire plan, including the very sacrifice of Jesus Christ, is an *utter failure* in bringing salvation to most of mankind, since most do not come to Christ. The Father and the Son are often portrayed as passively standing by patiently, hoping against hope that men and women will take them up on what they consider to be their wonderful offer of eternal life. But this is not the picture we find in John 6:37. The Son does not teach what is heard from too many pulpits today. The Father and the Son powerfully and unfailingly accomplish their desires, and are *completely able* to bring each and every elect one unto salvation.

"To Me"

The elect ones are the "believers" that come to Christ. They *know* their Lord, they *know* their Savior. They are not deceived by false prophets, they do not follow after false Christs. "The sheep follow him because they know his voice. And a stranger they will not follow, but will flee from him, because they do not know the voice of strangers... I am the good Shepherd, and I know My own, *and My own know Me*" (John 10:4-5,14). There is a relationship— personal knowledge between The Redeemer and the redeemed. Christians are such only because they are called efficaciously to come unto Christ.

It is often alleged by those who rebel against this truth that to believe in the absolute predestination and electing work of God, which is so clearly taught in these (and many other) passages, is to dehumanize man to the level of mind-numb "robots" or "automatons." "*You think man is like a puppet on a string*" they accuse. Surely, we must recognize that much of this kind of reaction comes from a rebellious heart, and not from a humble, contemplative reflection upon the truth. Yet, the charge is frequently made all the same. If we are committed to proclaiming the truth how are we to answer this?

Jesus' words at this point are highly instructive. The believer is not called to accept some abstract concept. He does not look for his eternal life in a system of belief, in an organization, a denomination, a specific church or creed. He is called to come unto the person called Christ. Jesus speaks of the believer coming "to Me." To truly come unto Jesus is personal and intimate by its very nature. Robots cannot have personal relationships. Puppets can never exercise faith. Automatons do not seek intimate communion with another. Only humans can come to Christ. Only mankind, the image-bearers of God can believe and trust in the Son, their creator.

We, as His sheep, *know* His voice. Have you ever had the experience of hearing the voice of a loved one that you had not seen for a long time? As soon as you heard the sound of that voice, your mind was filled with memories and emotions, was it not? If hard feelings persist from your last meeting, a quickening of the pulse and a shortness of breath results from hearing that voice. When all is well and you have longed to be with this person once again, isn't it true that everything else becomes unimportant, all projects are dropped, and you rush to greet this person? Knowing someone's voice implies communion, communication, familiarity, and fellowship, in other words— relationship. We know Christ's voice, because a relationship exists between us. He knows us, and we know Him. His perfect knowledge of us, however, precedes our incomplete knowledge of Him, and our knowledge flows from His.[20] Christians come to Christ, their Head, their Shepherd, their Lord. Their relationship, most certainly, is based solely upon the initiative and decree of God Himself. This does not mean that it is not a *personal* relationship, a *true* relationship, as full as any that we as created beings can experience. Far from thinking that the Christian faith as just "dead theology," recognizing the complete sovereignty of God in saving us through Christ Jesus is the sole and necessary foundation for our living relationship with Him.

So we see that the first clause of John 6:37 presents to us the King of Creation giving to the Son a gift of love. The result of this is that all who are so infallibly given, without question, will come to Christ in faith. In the rest of this verse we shall hear further comforting words from the Lord Jesus Christ.

3

Christ and the Christian

While Christ is the foundation, the root, head and husband of his people, while the word of God is Yea and Amen, while the counsels of God are unchangeable, while we have a Mediator and High Priest before the throne, while the Holy Spirit is willing and able to bear witness to the truths of the Gospel, while God is wiser than men, and stronger than Satan, so long the believer in Jesus is and shall be safe. Heaven and earth shall pass away, but the promise, the oath, the blood, on which my soul relies, affords me a security which can never fail.

—*John Newton*

Over the past century it has become fashionable to judge the success or failure of a particular ministry or minister on the basis of "numbers." How many are being "saved" many ask. How full is the altar on Sunday morning? How many are in Sunday School or on the church rolls?

Is giving up or down? The Christian Church, in America at any rate, has become thoroughly "success-oriented," and the measurements of this success have come to us directly from Wall Street and Madison Avenue.

One of the results of this newly found mentality is that the Gospel has been softened and watered down; made as "offense free" as possible, that way they can keep their "numbers" coming. This process has created some very, very strange concepts indeed. One of the most intriguing is to be seen in many conservative, "Bible-believing" churches in the land. It is just this: the church (its preacher) denies the ideas that God chooses some to be saved, denies that God's grace is completely effective for bringing about the salvation of men, and denies that Christ died solely and only for the elect. Yet at the same time will teach with utter sincerity, that once a believer is saved, he cannot lose his salvation! "Once saved, always saved!" they cry.

So what is so odd about this, you ask? Well, simply put, it makes absolutely no sense. If it was man's decision to get involved with this whole concept of Christianity, and God was helpless to save him without his cooperation and help, then why, having entered into the bargain, can he not just up and quit? If it was my decision to join up, why can't I also decide when I want to get out? If man had a part in saving himself, he is highly likely to mess up somewhere down the road, and so lose his salvation, or to decide he doesn't like the living arrangements for eternity after all, and to make other arrangements of his own.

Do not be mistaken! We believe that every man who is the object of God's saving grace, for whom Christ died as The Perfect Substitute, who is regenerated by the Holy Spirit, indwelt by that Spirit, justified by the blood of Christ The Lamb, and adopted into the family of God (all actions undertaken solely and completely by God Himself), will, without fail, receive eternal life and be saved! We believe in the perseverance of the saints without question. But it is why we believe in the perseverance of the saints that differs so tremendously from the above scenario. The saints will persevere in faith simply because their salvation is the perfect work of God. He is accomplishing His will in their lives, and therefore they will be true Christians— men and women who seek their all in Christ, and who will truly "persevere to the end," *not* as a way that they can *earn* salvation, but simply *because of the salvation they have already been given*! The person who has been saved by God is the only one who *can and will* persevere to the end!

We saw in the first phrase of John 6:37 the sovereignty of God in salvation. He, as the ruler of all men, gives some men to His Son, this results always in their coming to Christ in faith. This is the first aspect to be understood, and it always must stand at the foundation of our understanding of God's work in our lives. The Christian who seeks to know his own heart knows that unless God had moved first, he would never have been saved. But Jesus did not stop there. He goes on in the next phrase to express the result of this sovereign act of God.

Initial Exegesis

"And the one coming to Me I will never cast out." We will again examine these words closely, but first we will present what seems to be the only possible meaning given by the text. We have seen that the "one coming" to Christ is the one who is given by the Father to the Son. This person believes in Jesus Christ as Lord and Savior. Christ denies, in the strongest possible language, that any such person that comes to Him could possibly, ever, be cast out. Note who speaks here— the Lord Jesus Himself denies that He will ever cast out one who comes to

Him in faith. "Nothing shall separate us from the love of God which is in Christ Jesus" is how Paul expressed it (Romans 8:38-39). Of course, we have already emphasized that the one "coming" is one who is always coming, not just the surface level professors who say "Jesus" a few times and then go from there. We are talking here about a true Christian, a true follower of Christ, one who has saving faith and trust in the Son as his Savior. Such a one will never be cast out, for there is only one with that authority, Jesus Christ Himself, and He promises never to do so. Few passages so clearly, so unequivocally present the doctrine of the full and final perseverance of the saints as these precious words from the Son of God.

"The One Coming"

This phrase simply repeats the subject of the preceding clause, and we have already examined the rich meaning seen in the description of the Christian as the one who "is coming" to Christ. But lest we overlook, in our proper zeal for the truth of the eternal nature and security of salvation, the danger of false profession, let us remark again that the tremendous promise that is here given, and which will be further amplified in the following verses, is *not* for those who do not truly trust, truly believe, and truly *follow* Jesus Christ. There is no foundation in this passage (or any in God's Word) for one who does not truly love Christ, does not truly desire to follow Him, to be with Him, to honor Him and to glorify Him, to claim "eternal security." Simply walking down an aisle, shaking a man's hand, praying a prayer, or being baptized in a baptistery is not necessarily the same as coming to Christ and believing in Him. Surely, many have truly come to Christ through a prayer, or in an evangelistic service. But the simple *performance* of these actions does not make us a Christian or obligate God to save us. A one-time faith is not saving faith, nor are strong feelings that last but a night the same as trusting Christ as Lord. Saving faith lasts; those who have this kind of faith are coming and believing in Christ. Only these will persevere. Only these can claim these wonderful words spoken by The Lord.

"To Me"

Once again we note briefly the centrality of Christ in the Gospel. The sole source from which this person seeks to derive spiritual drink is Jesus Christ. This person does not bring the rags of his own "good works" to Christ, asking that Christ allow him to help save himself. He does not think that Christ is but a supplement, an addition to his own works of "righteousness." The one who comes to Christ seeks in Christ his all, his full sufficiency, and knows that the Son of God, the perfect Savior, can meet his every need.

"I Shall Never Cast Out"

Each language provides ways of expressing a negative, a denial. In French, the verb is often placed between the two terms "ne pas," so that one would say "I do not ask" , "Je ne prie pas" or "Je ne demande pas." In German, the word "nicht" is used, so that if one wished to say "I am not traveling to Hamburg today" one would say, "Ich fahre nicht heute nach Hamburg." However, if one wishes *to emphatically deny* something, or express a *strong negation*, most languages have a means of communicating this stronger statement. In French, instead of just using the "ne pas" form, one could use "ne jamais," which would give you the sense of "never." In German, another mode can be used to express the same idea.

Why the short discussion of languages? In English, we understand that placing two negatives together in one sentence not only results

in a poor sentence, but it also does not accomplish anything; that is, two negatives do not
strengthen the denial, and often end up creating
a positive! We find other ways of expressing
a strong negative statement. But the Greek in
which John wrote his Gospel is different from
English, French, or German. Two negatives *do*
strengthen one another, and, when put together
with a particular tense and mode, provide the
strongest means for expressing a denial, particularly of a future event, in the Greek language.[21]
And it is just this form that we find in the words
under our present consideration.

"I shall never cast out." Literally, the Greek
reads, "the one coming to Me no, never shall I
cast out." The language emphatically denies that
it is at all possible that the Lord Jesus would
ever, *ever* cast out one who comes to Him for
refuge, one who trusts in Him for salvation.
There simply is no possibility of this taking
place. Christ here gives His word, His promise,
His surety to those weary souls who come to
Him for rest: I will never turn you away, I will
never cast you out once I have given you refuge.
With me there is no "shadow of turning."

Eternally secure in Jesus Christ. The
Christian finds these words to be worth more
than all the gold in the world. But these words,

dear friend, come immediately *after* a strong, inescapable proclamation of the sovereignty of God in saving men. Great promises are normally founded upon strong doctrine. This is no exception. One cannot logically believe in the perseverance of the saints without first believing in the electing grace of God. We are secure because God wills it so. God's plan will be worked out, and that includes the salvation of the elect and their perseverance in faith. God is conforming us to the image of His Son, and since it is His will that our faith persevere, that we undergo sanctification, that we bring forth good works, then we shall. God does not draw men unto Christ for no purpose, nor is God incapable of accomplishing His desires (Psalm 135:6). Every Christian remains in the faith because the faith that is his is supernatural, a gift of God's grace.

Christ will never cast us out. But why? Why is the Son of God so intent upon making this strong statement. What is our surety? The word of the Lord certainly is enough, but like a generous King who lavishes His servants with blessings unimaginable, so our Lord continues His discourse, giving us a glimpse into the will of the Father for the Son, and how this gives us even greater confidence (if such is possible) in our relationship with Him for eternity.

4

The Son Doing the Will of the Father

I always do the things that are pleasing to Him.
—The Lord Jesus, John 8:29

"For I have come down from heaven, not in order to do My own will, but the will of Him who sent Me; and this is the will of the one who sent Me: that of all which He has given Me I lose nothing, but raise it up at the last day. For this is the will of My Father: that all the ones looking upon the Son and believing in Him might have eternal life, and I will raise him up at the last day.

—John 6:38-40

Some things are so self-evident that to express them elicits such kind response as "my, how profound!" Yet, we human beings are likely to forget about such self-evident things, and miss obvious conclusions and truths on that basis. The truth that is expressed in the words of Christ in John 6:38 is, for those who trust in Christ, and who make a practice of listening to His words on a regular basis, a self-evident one. Nothing could be less arguable and more obvious than the fact that the Son does the will of the Father. The idea that the Son would *ever disobey*, or seek His own will over the Father's will, is so ridiculous, that the mind of the believer automatically recoils at the thought.

Yet, we must also remember that Jesus often expressed His absolute submission to the will of the Father in contexts of demonstrating the unity that exists between the Father and the Son. Throughout the Gospel of John, a perfect balance is presented regarding the Person of Christ. What is meant by this is that when the high, exalted claims of Christ are presented, we also find His own declaration of His unity with, and submission to, the Father. When the deity of Christ is taught, as it is in such passages as John 5:17-18, or 10:28-30, soon we hear the Lord Jesus emphasizing the essential *unity* of the Father and the Son, and the Son's dependence upon the Father as the Son of Man, the Servant of God. Why is this? Surely the reason is that the Son wishes to make it quite clear that He is not a "maverick" going out on

His own, pursuing His own goals rather than those of the Father. There is only one God, not two, and since both the Father and the Son are described as God, and are divine Persons, there must be full and complete unity between them. It is inconceivable that there would be strife, tension, or disunity in the Godhead.

The Son does the will of the Father in all things. He came down from heaven to do the Father's will. We should not think that He was coerced or manipulated to do this, as if it was against His own will. Certainly not. When Paul describes that great action of humility wherein Christ laid aside His robes of glory and became flesh for our sakes, to suffer and die in our stead,[22] he makes it quite clear that Jesus was in full accord with the Father's desires, and that He humbled *Himself*— it was a voluntary action on Christ's part. The Son *always desires* to do the Father's will, to be the obedient Servant of God. The Father loves the Son and the Son loves the Father, and shows this love in His humble obedience to the Father.

So we see that the Son came down from heaven to do the will of the Father. And what was the will of the Father for the Son? What was God's intention in sending Christ? We need not wonder or guess, for Christ tells us plainly.

The Will of the Father for the Son

"And this is the will of the one who sent Me: that of all which He has given Me I lose nothing, but raise it up at the last day." We are privileged indeed to be given a glimpse into the eternal plan of the Father and Son in accomplishing the salvation of the people of God! God certainly did not have to reveal such wonderful truths to us, but He has, and we should never cease to be thankful for such a treasure that has been entrusted to us, such a wonderful comfort that these words provide.

The will of the Father for the Son— that which brought the eternal Son down from heaven to walk amongst us— is that the Son should lose *nothing* of what the Father has given to Him; but rather, is charged with the awesome responsibility of raising up at the last day all those who have been given unto Him. This is His task, His duty, His act of self-sacrifice and obedience to the Father. It is both positive and negative; He is not to lose any man that has been given into His care. These are the same men spoken of in verse 37, those who infallibly come to Christ as Lord. And how does He accomplish this? By completing their salvation; by raising them up at the last day, or as we will see in verse 40, by giving them eternal life. In short, the Son is *not* charged with simply securing a hypothetical *possibility of salvation* for the elect, but with actually *saving completely* those who are the objects of God's loving grace.

What does this entail? We know from the entirety of sacred Scripture that God is a holy God, and that nothing which is impure can stand before Him in heaven. Therefore, Christ is charged with providing *all of salvation* for His people. They must be cleansed, made holy, pure and spotless. God does not raise up to eternal life those who are condemned and guilty. The unrighteous are vile in His sight, and they will not receive from Him eternal bliss. Yet Christ is given these men, and charged with their salvation. How will He accomplish this?

Of course, we know how Christ does this. As The Good Shepherd, He lays down His life for the sheep, dying as their substitute, taking all their sins upon Himself. The Father then imputes to His people the righteousness of Christ, so that we stand forever before God holy and pure in His sight, not due to anything we have done, or because of anything we are in ourselves, but solely because of the work of Jesus Christ in our behalf. Christ is our all. He is everything to the Christian. He fills all, is in all, and He is our life (Colossians 3:4, 11). It is in Him that all the treasures of wisdom and knowledge are hidden (Colossians 2:3). He is the author and finisher of our salvation, the one who starts it, works it out, and completes it (Hebrews 12:2). This is as the Father wanted it. He places His people in the hands of the Son, having joined them to the Son in a supernatural union, so that the Son, by His perfect life of obedience, and perfect act of self-sacrifice upon the cross, can bring about their full and complete salvation.

There can be no room for boasting, as Paul told us in 1 Corinthians 1:30-31, for we did not place ourselves in Christ, we were placed there by the Father's decision. God did not choose us in Christ for anything we had done or would do. He chose us solely on the basis of His grace and mercy. We cannot seek any further answer as to why we are saved than God's grace. He who seeks such information shows a brashness that is not proper for a child of God. The work of our salvation is not our own. We are totally and completely dependent upon another— the Son of God. But can we think of anyone upon whom we would rather rely? Hardly! We have the security of knowing that our salvation, rather than being dependent upon us, is dependent upon Christ! What a wonderful foundation for the Christian in this storm-tossed world— the *true* immovable rock.

Christ is charged with the salvation of His people. Now let us consider, for only a moment (for the thought is too absurd to linger long in our minds), the position of those who assert that one can be truly a child of God, united with Christ, placed into the hands of the Son, and yet still end up under the wrath of God, lost for eternity, damned. There are many who teach that the Christian can cease being a Christian. Most of them, at the very least, are consistent in teaching that God has not chosen a specific people, but simply offers salvation to all, and leaves the ultimate decision up to man. We have seen how contradictory such a thought is to the Lord Jesus' teaching in this passage, and certainly we must understand that this entire perspective is based upon beliefs that strike at the heart of the Gospel— such ideas as the death of Christ being in vain, as it was (supposedly) made for so many who will end up as lost in hell for all eternity. But, aside from these things, let us take this teaching and examine it in the strong light of John 6:39. What must we conclude?

If one teaches that a true Christian can fail to be raised up at the last day, fail to receive eternal life, then it must be understood that such a person is teaching— even if in ignorance— that the Son of God can *fail* to do the will of the Father! Consider well what we are saying. If the true believer can fail to receive salvation, then it must be said that the Son has failed to do the very thing that the Father sent Him from heaven to accomplish, that being the salvation of His people! Preposterous? Indeed! But is this not what we must conclude, if indeed any man who comes to Christ can be lost? How might the Son fail to do the will of the Father? It seems that those who teach such an "eternal insecurity" would have to allege one of the following things: first, the Son is *not capable* of bringing men unto salvation *infallibly*. This is the common position, for it is alleged that the Son certainly *desires* to save men, but is then thwarted in His desire by the (ostensibly) almighty will of the creature! But we have already seen that Jesus teaches no such thing. Secondly, it might be alleged that the Son fails to do the expressed will of the Father because He is disobedient to the Father. We can dismiss that one immediately. So, if Christ is fully obedient, and, as the Second Person of the Trinity, is powerfully capable of accomplishing the task assigned to Him, then it must follow without question that Christ will accomplish His task. He will save *for all eternity, every single individual* who is given to Him by the Father, *infallibly*. So there is no possibility whatsoever that Christ will fail in His mission.

We may acknowledge that those honestly confused by such warning passages as Hebrews 6:4-6 and 10:28-30[23] may not *purposefully* intend to bring reproach upon the ability of Christ as Savior of men; but given the importance of this subject, we *must* point out that while this may not be their *intent*, it *is* the *result* of their teaching nonetheless. We therefore see the absolute necessity of *first* answering the question "Who saves— God or man?" *before* we can ever ask questions about eternal security. Only by answering the first question can we determine the answer to the second.

All Christians can confidently declare that it is God who saves men. That is the true Gospel. These have a personal relationship with Christ, and look to Him as Lord, and as Savior. We move now to consider the next words of Jesus to the (by this point) stunned crowd in Capernaum.

How A Person Displays True Faith

The will of the Father *for the Son* is that He raise up to eternal life all those who are given to Him, and who, as a result, come to Him in faith. Now Jesus announces the Father's will in a more general sense, by stating that all the ones looking and believing on the Son should have eternal life. The thrust of the passage is quite simply that it is the Father's will that Christ be the Savior of mankind. It is through the Son that the gift of eternal life is to be dispensed. Every man, woman, or child who looks upon Christ, who believes in Him, receives eternal life.

Of course, we have already seen men who "saw" the Lord Jesus, who observed His miracles and heard His teaching, yet they did not believe. The looking or gazing that is here described is again united with faith. It is a gaze of faith, a look of trust that brings eternal life. And, again, these are present-tense, ongoing actions. The believer's eyes are riveted to Christ and Him alone.

The proper balance is always maintained in the Word. First comes the action of God, which is always prior to the actions of man. In *response* to the work of God, man looks on Christ, believes on the Son, and receives eternal life *as a gift*. Looking and believing do not merit eternal life; there is nothing meritorious about looking in faith upon Christ. This is simply the means by which God has decreed to bring men to salvation. We are justified by faith, and by faith alone, for the simple reason that since Christ is Savior, and He is perfect in His work, there is nothing in the works of man that could possibly be added to the work of Christ!

Yet, every Christian will indeed look to Christ alone, and will believe on Him. God's gift of faith will accomplish that which He intends it to accomplish. It will be a living faith, one that works in love. Just as Christ will, without fail, save all the people of God, so too He will not fail to enable men to look and believe upon Him.

5

Human Inability

Wherefore, "Free-will" is nothing but the servant of sin, of death, and of Satan, doing nothing, and being able to do or attempt nothing, but evil!

*—Martin Luther,
The Bondage of the Will (1525)*

Martin Luther thought that one of the most significant works he ever wrote was the book, *The Bondage of the Will*. In this work Luther engaged the great humanist scholar, Desiderius Erasmus, in the ages-old debate over the ability, or inability, of the human will. Is the will free, or has it been enslaved by sin, incapacitated in its ability to truly do good? Luther and Erasmus were not the first to debate the subject, and each generation rekindles the conflict anew.

Truly, many modern interpreters of Luther have missed the centrality of this issue in his thought. It is one thing to misinterpret Martin Luther; but it is quite another however to misinterpret the Lord Jesus Christ. The former simply means you'll end up not fully understanding and appreciating the teachings of a great theologian of some centuries ago. The latter can result in misunderstanding He who is Truth incarnate.

> "Therefore the Jews were grumbling concerning Him, because He said, "I am the bread which came down out of heaven." And they said, "Is this not Jesus, the son of Joseph? Do we not know His father and His mother? Therefore How does He say, 'I came down out of heaven.'?""

The Lord Jesus' words fall on deaf ears though, surely a fulfillment of what He had just taught about man's dependence upon God to give him unto Christ. They are stuck upon the basic revelation of His heavenly origin. How can this man be from heaven when we know His father and mother? There seems to be a lull in the conversation, or at least enough time for some grumbling to take place, so that the Jews can begin discussing amongst themselves the divine claims made by Jesus.

It is probably a mistake to read these words with simply a sense of confusion on the part of the Lord's hearers. They were "grumbling concerning Him." It is not that they didn't understand what He was saying, but that they did not like what He was saying! Their words are soaked in unbelief and rebellion. Their questions are not really questions, but denials in disguise. That truly is a common ploy— most do not give open expression to disbelief in Christ. They hide the true rebellion of their heart under supposedly honest questions and "concerns." But the Lord Jesus cannot be taken in by their inquisitive smokescreen. He knows their hearts, and points out their *real* problem.

> "Jesus answered and said to them,"Do not grumble among yourselves! No one is able to come to Me unless the Father, who sent Me, draws him, and I will raise him up at the last day" (John 6:43-44).

Christ exhorts His listeners to stop their grumbling. Of course His words are offensive to them! They are offensive to *anyone* who has not been given by the Father to the Son. Then Jesus explains their disbelief in terms that are stark and clear. In a single verse the Lord dispels forever every system of works-salvation ever devised. Any concept of human merit is destroyed, any idea that man is the captain of his own salvation obliterated. How? Jesus tells us exactly what man *cannot do.*

"No Man is Able to Come to Me"

Does each and every man have the capacity, if he can exercise his own will, to come to God? Not if these words of Christ mean anything at all. Jesus minces no words here. The term He uses is a term which speaks to *ability.* "No man is able." The Lord negates the possibility that any man has the capacity, in and of Himself, to come to Christ. No man is able to *force or obligate* the Father to give him to the Son. In his sinful natural condition man does not have the ability to come to Christ and therefore never will.

This is a radical teaching in today's world. We live in a time when man thinks that his capacities and abilities are nearly limitless. Humanism, fallen mankind's religion, flourishes all around us. It teaches— "If you believe it, you can achieve it!" And in the midst of all of this, the Lord of heaven and earth flatly states, "No man is able to come to Me." Human *non*-ability. A shattering blow to the ego, and a truth that only the redeemed heart knows too well to be true. The man who has never had a glimpse of the glory and holiness of God, and the attendant realization of his own profound sin and vileness, has absolutely no basis upon which to understand Christ's words in this passage. They are truly "foolishness" to the one who has never known the depth of his own sin.

Might we be misinterpreting Christ's words? Is there any other way to understand Him? We have seen that he is replying to the grumbling of the Jews. They will not believe what He is saying to them. So the context supports the clear meaning of the text. But what about this term translated "able" ?[24] Could we be missing what it really means?

We could certainly find enlightening examples of the use of this term outside of John's writings.[25] But we shall limit ourselves primarily to John's own use of the term. The same phraseology[26] is found in Nicodemus' words in John 3:2— "We know that you are a teacher come from God, for *no one is able* to do these signs which you do, except God is with him." Jesus' response to Nicodemus in the next verse borrows the same phrase, for He says, "Unless a man is born from above, *he is not able* to see the kingdom of God." Man's inability to even see the Kingdom of God (much less decide to enter into it!) is found in this, one of the most often read passages on salvation in all of the Bible! John 3:6 continues, "Unless a man is born of water and the Spirit,[27] *he cannot enter into the Kingdom of God.*" Note that in each instance, the action *by God* (*born from above, born of water and the Spirit*) happens before the action of man, and is the only reason a man becomes able to see, or enter into, the Kingdom of God! Surely the Lord Jesus is consistent with this in John 6:44!

Elsewhere in John's Gospel, we hear Christ speaking of men being *unable* to go where He is going, speaking of His returning to the Father.[28] Surely no man has the capacity, simply by the exercise of his will, to enter into heaven (man's abilities are limited in this regard). In the eighth chapter, verse 43 we read, "Why do you not understand what I am saying? Because you *are not able* to hear My word." Here Jesus is addressing the same issue as in John 6:44. Why can't men "hear His word" and accept it? Because they are *not able* to hear His word and accept His message. As the Lord said a few verses later in John 8:47, in direct parallel with our passage in the sixth chapter, "The one who is from (or "of ") God hears the words of God; this is why you do not hear: you are not from (or "of ") God!"

Other passages that give the same meaning are John 10:29, where no one "is able" to snatch the people of God out of the hand of the Father, John 10:35, where the Lord says that the Scriptures "are not able" to be broken, and quite significantly John 12:39, where it is directly asserted that men *could not believe because God had blinded their eyes!*

Therefore, on the basis of even this brief survey of the term "ability" in John's Gospel, we are forced to conclude that Jesus meant exactly what we first asserted: no man has the ability to come to Him. But why? Why is man incapable of doing the right, proper thing? Surely if man were not under the dominion of sin, he would be able to see the glory of Christ, and would come to Him gladly, would he not? Yet, this does not take place. Many men curse Christ, and mock His name. Why, when coming to Christ would be a good, holy and just thing?

First, we need to remember the Lord's words to the Jews in John 8:31-32: "If you abide in My word, truly you will be My disciples; and you will know the truth, and the truth will make you free." Those who do not know truth are not free. Yet, truth is in Christ, in His word. Jesus spoke these words to men who had "believed" in Him; yet, their response makes it quite clear that they had only a surface faith, not the true, saving faith that comes only from God. As soon as they heard these words of the Lord, they reacted violently, denying that they had ever been enslaved! One who denies that he has ever been a slave to sin knows nothing of the redemption that is in Christ! As soon as His hearers rebel against His claims, the Lord reminds them, "Every one doing sin is a slave of sin." All sinners are enslaved, bound to sin. Why do we hear so much about "free will"? Why are people far more concerned about human freedom than the freedom of God? Because we have such little sense of our sin. If we knew the truth, we would know our bondage. Christ's word shows us the truth, and therefore sets us free.

The Bible tells us that "natural man," that is, the man who has not been born-again by the Spirit of God, does not understand the things of the Spirit of God (1 Cor. 2:14), but rather believes them to be complete foolishness. Furthermore, we are told that no man will seek after God (Romans 3:11), and that no man can ever do good who is by nature accustomed to doing evil (Jeremiah 13:23). The universal condition of man is a sad thing indeed. Because of this, Paul taught (Romans 8:5-9) that those who are "according to the flesh" are *incapable* of submitting to the law of God, and those who are the enemies of God are *incapable* of doing what is pleasing to Him. Obviously, coming to Christ is a pleasing thing in God's sight. So we see again, the universal testimony of the Scriptures, that God's gracious act of releasing us from the bonds of sin, and making us, who were once spiritually dead,[29] spiritually alive— is an absolutely necessary *prior to* any action of man.

"Unless..."

If we stopped here, we would surely have a dismal picture. Man is totally unable to save himself. He cannot even come to Christ for salvation outside of God's action, so desperately lost is he. But the Lord Jesus teaches us that the only ones who come to Christ are those who are drawn by the Father. No others come, for no others are able to come. There is no such thing as a Christian who is not one of the elect, one of those given unto the Son by the Father, and drawn by the Father unto the Son.

God draws those that He gives to the Son. What is the nature of this "drawing"? We can gain some understanding by noting the repetition of the thought of this verse later, in verse 65, where we read, "Because of this I said to you that no one is able to come to Me except it is given to him by the Father." Some translations speak of the Father "enabling" men to come to the Son. Jesus is clearly referring back to verse 44 when He says this, so then the "drawing" is restated in terms of it "being given to them" or of the Father's "enabling" men to come to Christ.

The term[30] is used in John 6:44, 12:32, and 21:6, 11. In the latter references it speaks of hauling a net, either into a boat, or up onto land. It speaks of a force being applied to move something from one place to another. But in John 12:32 Jesus speaks of His crucifixion "drawing all men" unto Himself. While many have used this verse to attempt to blunt the force of John 6:44, hoping to find here a "wooing" idea rather than the sovereign call of the Spirit of God in a person's life, just *the opposite* is to be found.[31] The cross was a symbol *of pain and death*. It could only repulse, not attract. For someone to be "drawn" because of the cross requires the supernatural activity of the Spirit of God. The death of Christ is beautiful only to those who are redeemed by it, who see in it the very power of God. Others see only an itinerant preacher dying miserably in shame. What is the difference between the two? The drawing of the Father. Furthermore, the context of John 12 forbids any softening of the words, as a quick glance at verses 37 through 40 demonstrate!

Others define this "drawing" by God as simply a benevolent enablement on His part that allows *all men* to come to some imagined "neutral point" from which they can freely decide whether they will, or will not, come to Christ. But is this a rational understanding? We can quickly see that this is not in harmony with what we have already seen in verses 37 through 40. Furthermore, it is inconsistent with the passage itself. Note that Jesus says, "...unless the Father... draws *him*, and I will raise *him* up at the last day." All who are drawn by the Father are also raised up by the Son! If *all* men are drawn, then *all* men will be raised up to eternal life! Since we have already seen that not all men are given by the Father to the Son (John 17:6, 9), then it follows that not all men are drawn to Christ by the Father.

There is only one way of salvation. Men are sinful rebels against God, by nature, enemies of holiness and He who is holy. Dominated by sin, ruled over by evil, we are helpless to even drag ourselves toward the true and holy God, even if we wanted to![32] We are dead in sin. "But God, who is rich in mercy, because of the the great love with which He loved us, even when we were dead in our transgressions, made us alive together with Christ" (Ephesians 2:4-5). The Father, in His infinite mercy and grace, saved us in Christ Jesus.

The Christian has been drawn unto Christ. Those who wish to boast in having something to do with their salvation, or who insist that the final decision lays with man, resist the clear meaning of Christ's word, "draw." But this is a wondrous term. It is beautiful to hear. *Drawn* in love. *Drawn* in mercy. *Drawn* unto the one who died in my place. It is a sovereign action, undertaken by the one who holds the entire universe together by His power. It is an irresistible drawing, most definitely, but it is a drawing of grace. The one drawing loves the one who is being drawn. And those drawn can never be thankful enough to God who brought them out of darkness into the marvelous light of Christ.

Hearing and Learning from the Father

Jesus Christ viewed the Scriptures as the final word in matters of authority. It is quite fitting that immediately upon uttering these tremendous words that we have been examining, He quotes the prophets[33] by stating, "And they shall all be taught by God." This He is obviously connecting with the drawing of the Father to the Son in the verse immediately preceding. Upon this basis, Christ then points out the fulfillment of this in the Father's leading men to Himself. He proclaims,— "All the ones hearing from My Father and learning, come to Me." The themes that Christ has sounded throughout John 6:35-44 are present here. *All* who hear and learn from the Father come. Not some, not most, but *all*. What is the source of their learning? The Father. He is the one who has given them to the Son, He is the one who charges the Son with their welfare, and He is the one who draws them unto Christ. And *how* does He draw them?— By teaching them. They hear[34] from the Father, and learn from the Father. Those who hear and learn infallibly, without question, do one thing: they come to Christ. Same theme, same teaching, expressed in different ways so as to develop fully the truths contained therein.

What does the Christian hear from the Father? Testimony to the Son. Jesus said, "And the Father who sent Me, that one has testified concerning me. You have never heard His voice or seen His form, and you do not have His word abiding in you, for you do not believe the one whom He sent" (John 5:37-38). The Father testifies concerning the Son, and He also teaches the truth about the Son. He shows the elect that Christ is worthy to be their Savior, and that they can trust in Him. This knowledge comes only from God. As Jesus told Peter upon his confession of Jesus as the Messiah, the Son of the living God, "Flesh and blood did not reveal this to you, but My Father, who is in heaven" (Matthew 16:17). Anyone who knows Christ knows Him because he has heard, and has been taught by, the Father.

6

Conclusion

God is glorified in the work of redemption in this, that there appears in it so absolute and universal a dependence of the redeemed on him.... Those that are called and sanctified are to attribute it alone to the good pleasure of God's goodness, by which they are distinguished. He is sovereign, and hath mercy on whom he will have mercy.... Hence these doctrines and schemes of divinity that are in any respect opposite to such an absolute and universal dependence on God, derogate from his glory, and thwart the design of our redemption.... However they may allow of a dependence of the redeemed on God, yet they deny a dependence that is so absolute and universal.

—Jonathan Edwards,
God Glorified in Man's Dependence

Every true follower of Jesus Christ desires to see Him be glorified and the Gospel proclaimed throughout the world. The Spirit of God prompts us to share the good news of the gospel with

79

all around us, for we know that this results
in the praise of the glory of God's grace, and
the glorification of our mighty Savior, Jesus
Christ. Truly, any man who has experienced
the cleansing and regeneration of the Spirit of
God knows the truth of Paul's teaching that the
gospel is "the power of God unto salvation."

God has determined, in His infinite wisdom,
to save through the proclamation of The Gospel
of Christ. Therefore, if we care about sharing
that message with others, our first and highest
priority should be the purity of that message.
We would never desire to *change* the Gospel,
would we? It is not our right to tailor the
message to our desires, our likes. The Gospel
comes from God, and He and He alone decides
what message we will proclaim to the world.

The problem is, God has already told us that,
from the world's view, the gospel is foolishness (1
Corinthians 1:18-31). Those who are perishing
will not find our message meaningful. They will
laugh, mock, and ridicule us for believing in
such silliness. How can the death of a Jewish
rabbi two thousand years ago have anything to
do with us today? And when we speak of men's
sin, we find out how quickly their laughter turns
to hatred. Christ is a stumbling block to the lost.
They are offended by His claims, offended by

His teaching. They do not want to hear about God's holiness, their sin, and their inability to save themselves. No man wishes to be reminded of how truly helpless he is, how completely dependent upon God he is.

As long as the Church desires only to please God, and not men, the world can mock both the gospel and those who believe it all they want. Our eyes are on Christ, and we seek only His glory. We will offend men with our declaration of God's absolute sovereignty and the total inability of man, just as Christ offended His hearers in Capernaum so long ago. Even those who had professed to follow Him turned away and left that day (John 6:66). Only the Twelve remained. Should we seek to do other than what our Lord did? Should we seek to compromise or soft-peddle, the message of God's work of salvation so that superficial followers will not be offended? Not if we seek God's glory.

Surely in our world today it is clear that a vast portion of that which considers itself a part of "Christendom" has stopped seeking the glory of God, and, having done so, has quickly rid itself of those aspects of the Gospel that are offensive to men. It is far more comfortable to proclaim only certain aspects of the truth, leaving that which might result in ridicule, mockery, or offense to the side. But truth cannot be divided up into sections at our whim. When we stop speaking in the way Jesus spoke in Capernaum, we no longer proclaim the gospel.

This book is written to Christians. From the outset we have said that our primary audience is the believer who truly desires to do that which is pleasing to the Father and which glorifies the Son. Working on that assumption, we have presented one of the clearest, strongest, and we feel least arguable, passages in all the teachings of Christ. We have sought to exegete the passages, taking care to deal honestly and openly with the words of Christ recorded for us in John 6:35-45. We have seen the tremendous consistency of the words of Christ, not only in this specific section of the text, but throughout all of the gospel of John, and then throughout all of the inspired Word. We have not isolated this passage from the rest of Scripture, thereby forcing upon it a foreign meaning and thrust. We have sought to allow the words of Christ to speak with their own authority, and to interpret themselves for us.

The result of this inquiry has been a strong proclamation of the following truths: first, the fact that God is sovereign, the owner and ruler of all things, including men. He is sovereign in all the affairs of men, including most especially their salvation. Secondly, we have seen the total inability of man to come to Christ outside of the Father's enablement. We have seen that men are not free, but slaves of sin until set free by Christ. In the third place, God's unconditional, free and sovereign election of men to salvation has been seen in His giving of a specific group, taken "from the world," to the Son. Next, in the fourth place, we have seen the Son's role as Savior of the elect. He is charged with bringing about their full and complete salvation. This He does by dying in their place so that they might stand before God robed in His perfect righteousness. Fifth, we have seen that those who are given to the Son cannot possibly fail to come to Him in faith. God's drawing of men unto Christ is irresistible. And finally, we have seen that Christ will never, ever cast out one who has come to Him for salvation. The saints *will* persevere in faith because they have a perfect Savior.

We believe strongly that these truths are not limited in their expression to this passage. In fact, some of these truths are to be found in even greater clarity in other parts of the Word of God. But the Bible, being the consistent, inspired revelation of God, will teach the same truths throughout. And it does. These are not unimportant issues. Jesus certainly did not think they were. In fact, He was willing to press them upon His hearers to the point of driving away all who did not have true faith. We must follow His example.

The Church today is filled to overflowing with men and women who find Christianity "convenient." Sadly, in our desire to build the big buildings, provide the flashy programs, and to "succeed" in the world's eyes, we have become dependent upon the good-will of the surface followers of Christ. Preach what Christ preached in Capernaum so long ago, and you will offend those people. They may not show up next Sunday. They may not give money this month. They may never come back. Others may call you a radical, an unloving dogmatist. But we are sure that they said the same about Christ, and Paul, and Peter, and John, and all those who loved the gospel of Christ. That did not stop them from proclaiming the truth. May God give us the boldness to offend those who need offending. Let us pray that God will purify His Church, and in so doing bring glory to His name.

Dear Christian, I exhort you to be submissive to the authority of Christ in His Word. If you have heard the words of Christ, as I pray that you have, then you must believe and act on that belief. I hope that you will thank God that in eternity past He decreed your salvation. I hope that you join me in praising the Father for His having given us to His Son, and charged Christ with our salvation. Our hearts should fill with thanks when we realize that when we were yet helpless, Christ died in our place. And what greater comfort can we have than to know that He who saved us is pledged to raise us up at the last day and give to us eternal life? Christ is our hope, our life, our joy. If He is yours, praise Him for what He has done for you.

It is my prayer that you have been blessed with me by this exploration into God's Holy Word. May the Spirit of God write upon our hearts His truth. May God bless you.

— James White

Endnotes

Chapter One

1) Matthew 14:22-33, Mark 6:45-51, John 6:45-51. The feeding of the five thousand is found in all four accounts, Matthew 14:13-21, Mark 6:32-44, Luke 9:10-17, and John 6:1-13. The events of this day remained vivid and clear in the minds of the disciples!

2) εγω ειμι

3) Isaiah 41:4,43:10,46:4, Haggai 1:13, etc.

4) See, for example, the Psalmist's struggle as recorded in the 73rd Psalm, and how he found peace in the place of worship, Psalm 73:17).

5) The Roman Catholic doctrine of the Eucharistic sacrifice of Christ certainly cannot find support in John 6, even though nearly every defender of Rome attempts to press it into service in that way.

6) As in John 3:16, 5:24, 6:35,37,40,47, etc.

7) Most often the present participle is used, as here in John 6:35, ερχομενος and πιστευων.

8) Specifically, Christ says that he who looks (a present participle indicating an ongoing action, not just a glance, but a continuing steady gaze) and believes (another present participle, e.g.:

continues believing) has eternal life. Those who do not look and keep on looking, believe and keep on believing, cannot put a claim on Christ for eternal life!

Chapter Two

9) Obviously, our entire discussion will be based upon the belief that the text of Scripture, being inspired revelation, is capable of such minute examination, and that the Word is self-consistent as a whole. The fact that such a high view of the Bible is not common today helps to explain why the strong theology and teaching of the Lord Jesus is not common as well.

10) This will come out most clearly in the discussion of verse 44.

11) God's grace is demanded to remove the blindness of sin, and if God does not give His grace to a man (and by definition, grace cannot be something which is demanded at any time), that man will remain in the disbelief that is the result of his own sin and rebellion.

12) The Greek term, παν, is neuter in gender rather than masculine. The relative pronoun that follows is neuter as well. The same is to be found in verse 39. The use of the neuter is best explained as considering all of the elect of God as a single whole. That individual persons

are in view as well is clearly seen by the fact that the actions undertaken by the "all," that of coming, looking, believing, etc., are all actions that individuals take. The elect as a whole come, look, and believe, in as much as each of the individuals who make up the whole elect has come, looked, and believed.

13) Nine words are used in the Greek.

14) And we should point out that many believers continue to struggle with this concept since we still have sin in our lives, and do not perfectly apply what we know to be true about God to our lives.

15) All summed up in manifesting the name of the Father.

16) Romans 8:33.

17) See above on John 6:35.

18) John 4:13-14.

19) It is often said that this decision is aided by God's grace, but even so, it is rarely confessed that this grace is anything more than an aid, let alone a divine power that actually accomplishes God's purposes.

20) God the Father chose us "in Christ Jesus" before the foundation of the world (Ephesians 1:4-6). Our union with the Lord Jesus is foundational to understanding all that God is doing in bringing about our full and complete salvation.

Chapter Three

21) We are referring to the "aorist subjunctive of strong denial" which uses the negative particle σου μη, the aorist tense and the subjunctive mode.

Chapter Four

22) Philippians 2:5-11.

23) These passages do not teach that it is possible for one who has truly been given by the Father to the Son to be lost, but rather teach that all those in the community of faith should take care and be watchful, as they themselves do not have infallible knowledge of their own hearts, let alone the hearts of others. There are many in the professing community who look like Christians but who are in fact doing little more than playing at religion.

Chapter Five

24) δυναται.

25) For example, Matthew 27:42 uses the term in saying, "He saved others, but he is not able to save Himself." The term's reference to ability is clear.

26) ουδεις δυναται.

27) Titus 3:5-7, 1 Corinthians 6:11, and Ephesians 5:26 show us that the washing that is mentioned

here is not any physical action, or any work performed by man. Instead, as we have seen in John 6, it is the sovereign action of God in drawing men to Christ, accounting them righteous in light of the virtue of Christ's work, justifying them in the blood of Christ (Romans 5:9).

28) Passages such as John 7:34,36, 8:21,22.

29 Ephesians 2:1-3, Colossians 2:13-14.

30) ελκω.

31) We cannot here go into depth in discussing the "all men" of 12:32.

We simply assert that the only consistent interpretation is to understand the all as meaning "all kinds" of men rather than "every single human being." This is consistent with John's teaching in 11:51-52.

32) Some might insist that they know of people who truly seek after God, but do not accept Christ. We submit that either these persons are under the influence of the Spirit of God, who will lead them to Christ, or they are seeking after the benefits of God, without actually having direct dealings with God. It is easy to understand a man seeking after a god who is less than the true God, but the Bible teaches that no man will seek after the Holy God unless he is first sought by God Himself.

33) Seemingly a conflate reading of Isaiah 54:13 and Jeremiah 31:34.

34) See again the use of this term in John 8:43, 47.

THE MISSION OF GREAT CHRISTIAN BOOKS

The ministry of Great Christian Books was established to glorify The Lord Jesus Christ and to be used by Him to expand and edify the kingdom of God while we occupy and anticipate Christ's glorious return. Great Christian Books will seek to accomplish this mission by publishing Gospel literature which is biblically faithful, relevant, and practically applicable to many of the serious spiritual needs of mankind upon the beginning of this new millennium. To do so we will always seek to boldly incorporate the truths of Scripture, especially those which were largely articulated as a body of theology during the Protestant Reformation of the sixteenth century and ensuing years. We gladly join our voice in the proclamations of— Scripture Alone, Faith Alone, Grace Alone, Christ Alone, and God's Glory Alone!

Our ministry seeks the blessing of our God as we seek His face to both confirm and support our labors for Him. Our prayers for this work can be summarized by two verses from the Book of Psalms:

> *"...let the beauty of the LORD our God be upon us,*
> *And establish the work of our hands for us; Yes, establish*
> *the work of our hands." —Psalm 90:17*

> *"Not unto us, O LORD, not unto us, but to your name*
> *give glory." —Psalm 115:1*

Great Christian Books appreciates the financial support of anyone who shares our burden and vision for publishing literature which combines sound Bible doctrine and practical exhortation in an age when too few so-called "Christian" publications do the same. We thank you in advance for any assistance you can give us in our labors to fulfill this important mission. May God bless you.

For a catalog of other great
Christian books
including additional titles
by James White
contact us in
any of the following ways:

write us at:
**Great Christian Books
160 37th Street
Lindenhurst, NY 11757**

call us at:
631. 956. 0998

find us online:
www.greatchristianbooks.com

email us at:
mail@greatchristianbooks.com

Printed in Great Britain
by Amazon